Simple Communication with God
Praying with Simplicity

Dawn Dixon, Ph.D.

Dante's Publishing • Atlanta, Georgia

Simple Communication with God
Praying with Simplicity

Copyright © 2011 by Dawn Dixon. All rights reserved

Unless otherwise indicated, all Scripture quotations are taken from the King James, Message or Amplified version of the Bible.
No portion of this publication may be duplicated, stored or transmitted in any form (electronically, photocopies, recordings, scanning, storage....) without written permission of the copyright holder, except as provided by United States Copyright Law.

Library of Congress Control Number: 2011935403
ISBN: 978-093871-5-2

For Information or additional copies of this book, contact
Dr. Dawn Dixon
773.852.3003

Simple Communication with God
Praying with Simplicity

Table of Contents

Acknowledgements...vi

Introduction...ix

Developing a Relationship with the Father...........................1

Purpose and Importance of Communicating......................15

Scriptures to Assist with Simple Communication................31

Let's Set the Atmosphere...49

Simple Prayers..65

Simple Prayer Declarations..77

About the Author...84

Acknowledgements

First, I would like to acknowledge my Heavenly Father, Almighty God, for allowing me to pen this information and share it so He can have communication with His children. I thank you Lord for gracing me with your wisdom.

In memory of my mom, Barbara J. Scales-Dixon, thank you for instilling in me the ability to believe in myself and to use what God has given me, despite obstacles that I must face.

I thank my father, Jesse Dixon, who constantly challenges me to put a prayer before the Lord for the simple needs of the family and to continue walking on this prayer journey.

Thanks to my beautiful children (Ori and Arielle) who continuously remind me to walk in what God has given me and to be "my best self" because others are waiting to receive what God has placed inside of me.

I thank Coach Sandra and Coach Rhonda "the Energizer" for reminding me there was a book inside of me waiting to be birthed. Thanks to both of you for your mid-wife skills!

I also thank all of the people across the United States who join me every Wednesday at 5:00 am for "Early Morning

Prayer with Dr. Dawn" and stand in the gap to pray for the needs of others.

I thank all the students who participated in the teaching class of "Simple Communication with God" and encouraged me that others needed to hear what was being taught. This class was life changing for those who felt like God didn't or wouldn't hear their prayers for one reason or another. I thank you for the PUSH!!

Special thanks to my Unveiling Roses Ministries family for keeping me lifted up and covered in prayer and allowing me to flow as the Holy Spirit leads in teaching and inspiring you to be all that God has called you to be.

Your Simple Communication with God CAN be the conduit for another individual's needs!

Introduction

Simple Communications With God is written for those of you who desire to communicate with God but feel you don't know how. I want to empower you with tools so that you can have a talk with God on a daily basis without fear. You will learn tips for talking with Him as though He was the only person ready to listen and give you the answer to your situation. He is omnipresent and a very present help in your time of need. You are special to Him and He is concerned about your every need. According to Psalm 138:8 ... "God wants to perfect those things which concerneth you."

For those of you who have a good rapport and trusting relationship with your parents...think about it this way: Imagine calling them on the spur of the moment and asking them to meet you at your favorite restaurant to discuss a private situation. They know everything about you (well almost, lol). You know you can count on them being on time to meet you at the designated place. Matter-of-fact, anytime you need them, you call and they avail themselves. They are never upset or disappointed about the things you share or with you as a person. They simply rearrange their schedule to be there for you. They listen and respond to you with love, respect and consideration.

For those of you who have a best friend or significant other and you are excited when you see him or her .... think about it this way: Imagine sitting and talking to him or her on a park bench in the summertime. You want to just pour your heart out about a specific situation and he/she will take the time to listen and not pass judgment on what you say. You feel comfortable and begin to talk without trying to find the right words or pronunciation; this is your best friend and he/she accepts you for who you are glitches and all with NO interruptions!

Everyone desires to have that special person to whom they can pour their hearts out without being judged, criticized or ostracized. We desire someone we can talk to without being interrupted and misunderstood. We just simply want to communicate and allowed to be ourselves. Many of us have found that we need to put on a false face in order to be accepted, understood or heard by others, which causes some of us to continue to hold on to painful, dark secrets.

Well, God can be the one we reveal these painful, dark secrets to. He's the one we can go to without being judged, criticized or ostracized. We can make Him our significant other and best friend. We can develop a trusting relationship with Him and begin to daily pour out our hearts to Him. We can communicate with God the same way we chose to communicate with our parents or significant other. Think about it this way...you have a dire need and your mom or best friend is unavailable. You can now make God your confidant/best friend/significant other whatever or whomever you need Him to be and discuss what's on your mind.

With God, you do not have to pretend to be someone else, you can just **Be Yourself!** It's a blessing to just be who God created you to be. No FALSE representation! You can talk to Him on your level and He can and will understand.

So I pray that *Simple Communication with God* leads you to develop a closer relationship with God and begin to apply some of the strategies so you can have daily, simple communications with God.

At the end of each section is an opportunity for you to journal your thoughts as well as write down important notes.

Say this prayer with me:

Father, God, I thank You for allowing this book to enter into my hands. I praise You for who You are and bless Your Name. I repent of my fear of communicating with You because I felt I didn't have the right words or format to present to You. Today, I turn this over to You and now I will begin to have simple communication daily just by talking to You the best way I know how. Your Word says that I am to pray without ceasing and I challenge myself to spend some quality time with You to discuss what's on my mind and then sit quietly to hear the instructions you give. It's a good thing to be able to come to your throne room and have confidence that You hear what I am saying. I thank you, Lord that I am free to pray without fear, doubt and disbelief. Thank You for teaching me your way. In Jesus' name I pray. Amen

Now let's get started.

Developing A Relationship With The Father

According to the World English Dictionary, the term "relationship" means: 1) the state of being connected or related; 2) association by blood or marriage; kinship and 3) the mutual dealings, connections, or feelings that exist between two parties, countries, people, etc.

The Merriam Webster's Learner's Dictionary describes the word "relationship" as: 1) the way in which two or more people, groups, countries, etc., talk to, behave toward, and deal with each other; 2) a romantic or sexual friendship between two people, and 3) the way in which two or more people or things are connected.

In today's society, we have an option to develop and form all kinds of relationships. We may choose to have interpersonal, casual, and/or intimate relationships. We develop and identify some as acquaintances, affiliations, companionships, significant others, memberships, family, extended family, play sisters/brothers and so forth. Almost everyone that we come in contact with can be put in one category or another. Some of these people we desire to know better than others and want to find our likes and dislikes and commonalities. Getting to know someone new requires spending time with them, dining with them, talking on the phone or doing other things together. If we find that we like the person, the greater our desire to get to know him or her, and the more time we will spend with them. God wants us to get to know Him more intimately. Getting to know and developing a relationship with Him requires us to spend more time in His presence. When we do this we learn to trust Him and learn His attributes, likes and dislikes. We also discover His plans for our lives. A fruitful relationship involves mutual giving and receiving.

Unlike a person you meet just for fun, the Father desires for us to commit to an intimate relationship with Him. He wants us to call on Him day and night no matter what's going on or how we feel. He welcomes us and can't wait to hear our voice. His arms are open wide and His ears never tire of hearing from us. He will never reject us or make us feel like we are bothering Him. He wants us to spend quality and quantity time in His presence.

We must first, however, establish our relationship through receiving Jesus as our Lord and Savior and getting to know HIM. Romans 10:9-10 tells us: "Because if you acknowledge and confess with your lips that Jesus is Lord and in your heart believe (adhere to, trust in, and rely on the truth) that God raised Him from the dead, you will be saved. For with the heart a person believes (adheres to, trusts in, and relies on Christ) and so is justified (declared righteous, acceptable to God), and with the mouth he confesses (declares openly and speaks out freely his faith) and confirms [his] salvation."

Jesus is our entrance to developing our relationship with the Father. He paved the path.

We can feel free to come into His presence without hesitancy

(Hebrews 4:16 "Let us therefore come boldly to the throne of grace that we may obtain mercy, and find grace to help in time of need). The veil has been torn in half by Jesus and we have an invitation to come on in.

Sometimes it is hard for people to accept that they can come into God's presence and they give all kinds of excuses why this is so....but according to Romans 5:9-11 (The Message Bible) and Romans 5:1-2 (Amplified Bible) we have a friendship and an invitation:

> **Romans 5:9-11:** "Now that we are set right with God by means of this sacrificial death, the consummate blood sacrifice, there is no longer a question of being at odds with God in any way. If, when we were at our worst, we were put on friendly terms with God by the sacrificial death of his Son, now that we're at our best, just think of how our lives will expand and deepen by means of his resurrection life! Now that we have actually received this amazing friendship with God, we are no longer content to simply say it in plodding prose. We sing and shout our praises to God through Jesus, the Messiah!" (emphasis mine)
>
> **Romans 5:1-2:** "THEREFORE, SINCE we are justified, acquitted, declared righteous, and given a right standing with God through faith, let us [grasp the fact that we] have [the peace of reconciliation to hold and to enjoy] peace with God through our Lord Jesus Christ (the Messiah, the Anointed One). Through Him also we have [our] access (en-

<u>trance, introduction) by faith</u> into this grace (state of God's favor) in which we [firmly and safely] stand. And let us rejoice and exult in our hope of experiencing and enjoying the glory of God." (emphasis mine)

You have been reconciled back into a righteous relationship with the Father through the blood of Jesus CHRIST. Your relationship with God should not be compared to your earthly relationships where you have been ignored, disappointed, lied to, hurt and/or misused. God is so different; he is ready to listen when you talk. He has no cell phone with limited minutes that he can't pick up for fear it will shut off. He does not drop calls or look at his caller ID and decide not to take your call when your name scrolls across the panel. He's not struggling to see whether you are calling long distance and if you are in His geographical phone payment plan. And, more importantly, He will not push the reject button to dismiss your call and send it to voicemail. Our God is available 24/7 to talk with us. He is waiting to hear His son's or daughter's voice any time of the day. He knows your tone. He knows what you are doing and not doing. He has called you His child and He knows YOU.

The above Scriptures prove that You can develop a strong relationship with the Father and it is available for you to do today.

God wants you to develop a personal relationship with Him. He wants your walk with him to be your lifestyle. He desires fellowship with you. He wants you to get to know Him. He wants you to have an internal and consistent lifestyle change that includes daily fellowship with Him. Your relationship must be consistent and developed to maturity over time. This relationship has to be cultivated. It is not religious or a traditional way of doing things. You must get to know God and His unfailing love for you through your intimacy.

So I invite those of you who haven't established a relationship with the Lord to do so today. Take time right now and get acquainted with Him so you can begin your simple communication and enhance your intimacy today. I guarantee this relationship will not be one-sided. It will be beneficial and fruitful. You will see a great positive change in your life. It's a relationship filled with benefits! Open up your heart and don't hold back your love to build this relationship, let Him in. It's a trusting and loving relationship that you can continually build on. Day after day, you will be able to watch your life change positively. Other people will recognize the change also.

This relationship is the beginning of your simple communication with God. It will open up new avenues for you and those around you. Take the time today and pursue your Father. Begin spending five minutes a day to build your relationship with God. You will increase the length of your prayer time as you continue to meet with Him each day. Your countenance will brighten; your attitude will become more positive; and your eyes will open!

(Examples of the types of relationships to build with God)

Develop a relationship where He's your Provider. Philippians 4:19 reads "And my God shall supply all your need according to His riches in glory by Christ Jesus." What are your needs today? Begin developing your relationship and trust God to supply every need you have whether it is big or small. God is able.

Develop a relationship where He's your Healer (in all areas). Where are you experiencing dis-ease? He will heal you everywhere you hurt. Isaiah 53:5 reads "But He was wounded for our transgressions, He was bruised for our guilt and iniquities; the chastisement [needful to obtain] peace and well-being for us was upon Him, and with the stripes [that wounded] Him we are healed and made whole."

Develop a relationship where He's Your Peace in the midst of your storms. What storm, trial or situation are you dealing with? Philippians 4:7 (Amp) reads "And God's **peace** [shall be yours, that tranquil state of a soul assured of its salvation through Christ, and so fearing nothing from God and being content with its earthly lot of whatever sort that is, that **peace**] which transcends all understanding shall garrison and mount guard over your hearts and minds in Christ Jesus." The King James version reads: "And the **peace** of God, which passeth all understanding, shall keep your hearts and minds through Christ Jesus."

Develop a relationship where He is your Protector. Do you need protection from all the chaos and cares of the world? Psalms 91:1-2 reads "He that dwelleth in the secret place of the most High shall abide under the shadow of the Almighty. I will say of the LORD, He is my refuge and my fortress: my God; in him will I trust". God will protect you and hide you under the shadow of His wings.

Develop a relationship where He is your Hiding Place. Do you want to find that hiding place where you can get away and rest, rejuvenate and be refreshed? You can rest in Him and rejuvenate your strength, your mind, your love, etc. **Psalm**

119:114 reads "Thou art my **hiding place** and my shield: I hope in thy word."

Take time and develop other areas where you want a relationship with the Father!

A FRUITFUL RELATIONSHIP

INVOLVES

MUTUAL
GIVING
AND
RECEIVING

IF SOMEONE ONLY TAKES FROM YOU...

AND NEVER ADDS ANYTHING

****

IT'S TIME TO REASSESS

For Your Review:

Take a moment and confess that Jesus is Lord of your life by repeating Romans 10:9-10.

After reading this section, please jot down your thoughts about Romans 5:1-2. Describe how your relationship with God is today.

Describe the ingredients of a fruitful relationship.

When should you reassess your relationships?

Name three ways you plan on developing or enhancing your relationship with God.

Read and write the Scriptures identified in this section that indicate you can have a relationship with God.

Write down three areas where you want to develop a relationship with God.

How do you plan on developing your relationship with God in these areas?

How did this section assist in developing your relationship with God?

Journal Your Thoughts:

Journal Your Thoughts:

Journal Your Thoughts:

Journal Your Thoughts:

Journal Your Thoughts:

Purpose and Importance of Communicating

The purpose of communicating is to share your thoughts and feelings with another person. This exchange could be with someone that you trust (whether public or private) to obtain feedback or input for some situation or you might just need to vent. This person is probably someone you know or have spent time with, and believe he or she has your best interest at heart. Your friend understands your personality traits, your behaviors and your attitudes. During communications, you are painting a clear picture of what's on your mind or simply expressing some inner/deeper emotions that you need to get outside of your head. She or he understands your style and allows you to be yourself. She or he will not spread your business or talk negatively behind your back even when the relationship goes bad. Neither will your friend cast judgment. She or he listens with an attentive ear and does not interrupt until you've completed your statement.

Remember, communication involves more than just you. It usually takes a second party. You talk and the other person listens. This exchange also happens in reverse; the other talks and you listen. This is the essence of true fellowship.

The definition of <u>communication</u> according to the World English Dictionary: 1) the act or an instance of communicating; the imparting or exchange of information, ideas, or feelings 2) something communicated, such as a message, letter, or telephone call.

You can have verbal and non-verbal communication. We spend time daily communicating and sharing information with people who can't help us and don't and won't support what we do. We pour out our ideas and it seems like we never said anything of importance. The conversation somehow turns from what you were saying to be about the person you were communicating with. They act as though it's all about them and "yes" you are beginning to feel that it's not worth sharing your thoughts any more. Soon we recognize (and sometimes we never do) that these individuals do not have our best interest at heart; neither are they interested in our destiny or where God is taking us. They want us to remain the same uninteresting and unproductive person they first met or so they thought. (Laughing as I write). They are not good listeners and their feedback is not what God wants you to hear most of the time.

It's time for us to switch our communication partner. We need a partner who is willing to listen and able to assist us as we encounter problems, issues, trials, situations and circumstances. We need to go to our listening and power source! We need to go to God the Father and pour out our hearts. He will listen and then speak peace in our situations and give strategies to move forward. He will also communicate to the hearts and minds of the people to whom we need to connect and orchestrate the crossing of our paths at just the right time to provide us an answer to our problem. God has all our answers.

Now I am not saying we don't need to communicate with others; I'm simply saying that when we go to our Source, He is able to lead us in the direction of those who can help us find a solution to our situation.

How many of you can think of an individual that interrupted you every time you would begin to speak or before you could finish your sentence; somehow they take over the conversation and it becomes all about them and their issue? (I'm laughing again.)

Most of the time, people are so preoccupied with their own issues, they don't have time to listen to us and they surely don't have an answer. They may have an opinion, but we need an answer. Sometimes, we just need someone to listen as we vent. We're not looking for anyone to give us feedback or say anything. We realize that sometimes we just need to get it out!

God has a listening ear. He will wait until we finish talking and then He'll speak back to us. But we must relax and wait! This is a good place for me to identify another synonym for communication: "PRAYER."

The definition of prayer according to the Merriam-Webster Dictionary *a (1)*: an address to God or a god in word or thought; *(2)*: a set order of words used in praying *b*: an earnest request or wish 2): the act or practice of praying to God or a god; and 3): a religious SERVICE consisting chiefly of prayers —often used in plural 4): something prayed for.

The term communication is similar to prayer. In prayer, we have usually identified our partner as God the Father!

The terms communication and prayer are interrelated. Once

we begin to communicate with God on a regular basis using simple communication, our prayer life will develop. This daily communication will cause us to have a better spiritual life and we'll become more empowered to handle issues/problems that we encounter every day. We are building a Godly and Spiritual relationship using simple communication!

Lives are changed, individuals are led by the Spirit or Word of God and our communities are affected and infected by people who know how to have simple communication with God. Every time a situation or need arises in our neighborhoods, our families, our friends or loved ones' lives, we will stop and have simple communication with God to learn strategies and obey the instructions that God gives to us. We will be equipped to share what God gives us to individuals so they can know that they can also have simple communication with God and get answers! Remember, your simple communication with God can be the conduit for another individual's needs!

Begin your simple communication today. God is waiting for you to communicate with Him. You can talk to Him about anything that concerns you. Tell Him your desires, tell Him your passions, tell him your concerns for your family and loved ones; tell Him your fears and tell Him your joys. He is available and ready to listen. All you have to do is simply communicate with Him using prayer as your tool! We can communicate with God by spending time in His Word and time in prayer. Communication with God can be done almost anywhere; in your car, in the bathroom, on your lunch breaks, walking, etc.

You can begin to communicate with Him and pour your troubles and or concerns on His shoulders. You can cry, laugh, or even scream, if you choose, and God will avail Himself to hear you.

The only thing you have to do is choose to meet with Him on a regular basis to share your thoughts. When you do this, you can expect Him to be there when you need Him.

God is available 24 hours a day, 7 days a week. He knows everything about you. He knows everything you've ever done and didn't do. Yet, He is still available when you call!

God beckons us to communicate with Him. Open yourself up and share your thoughts. God is waiting to hear from you!

> Jeremiah 29:12-13: "Then you will call upon Me and go and pray to Me, and I will listen to you. And you will seek Me and find Me, when you search for Me with all your heart."
>
> Jeremiah 33:3: "Call to me and I will answer you. I'll tell you marvelous and wondrous things that you could never figure out on your own."
>
> Isaiah 55:6: "Seek the Lord while you can find him. Call on him while he is near."

God Knows YOUR voice.....

He is waiting

on You

to Talk

to HIM

Synonyms For Communication

ARTICULATION

CORRESPONDENCE

CONNECTION

CONVERSATION

EXPRESSION

DISSEMINATION

MAKING KNOWN

MESSAGE

PRAYER

TELEPHONE CALL

UTTERANCE

For Your Review:

How do you define communication?

Who do you communicate with daily?

Do these individuals interrupt you when you talk?

How do you feel when you're interrupted?

Do you need to change your communication partner? Explain.

Describe your desire to communicate with God.

Do you believe God knows your voice and tone?

What types of thoughts would you like to share with Him?

Share your personal thoughts on the Scripture Jeremiah 33:3.

Write a brief summary of how you want to enhance your daily communication with God.

Journal Your Thoughts:

Journal Your Thoughts:

Journal Your Thoughts:

Journal Your Thoughts:

Journal Your Thoughts:

Journal Your Thoughts:

Simple Communication with God

Journal Your Thoughts:

YOU HAVE BEEN GIVEN

A PERSONAL INVITATION

TO COMMUNICATE

WITH THE FATHER

Hebrews 4:16

"Let us then fearlessly and confidently and boldly draw near to the throne of grace (the throne of God's unmerited favor to us sinners), that we may receive mercy [for our failures] and find grace to help in good time for every need [appropriate help and well-timed help, coming just when we need it]."

Will You Accept?

Scriptures To Assist With Simple Communication

There are several Scriptures in the Bible where we are invited to communicate with God. Read and repeat out loud the following Scriptures: After repeating them, you should be assured that you can have the right to have simple communication with God using the tool of prayer. Amen! (If not, please reread the Scriptures until they penetrate your spirit man and you know that you know that you know that God loves you and has an open door policy for you to communicate with Him).

> *Thus says the LORD who made it, the LORD who formed it to establish it (the LORD is His name): "Call to Me, and I will answer you, and show you great and mighty things, which you do not know." (Jeremiah 33:2-3)*
>
> *"And whatever things you ask in prayer, believing, you will receive." (Matthew 21:22)*
>
> *"Do not be anxious about anything, but in everything by prayer and supplication with thanksgiving let your requests be made known to God." (Philippians 4:6)*
>
> *"And in that day ye shall ask me nothing. Verily, verily, I say unto you, whatsoever ye shall ask*

the Father in my name, he will give it you. Hitherto have ye asked nothing in my name: ask, and ye shall receive, that your joy may be full". (John 16:23-24 KJV)

"The LORD is near to all who call upon Him, to all who call upon Him in truth". (Psalm 145:18)

"Now this is the confidence that we have in Him, that if we ask anything according to His will, He hears us. And if we know that He hears us, whatever we ask, we know that we have the petitions that we have asked of Him."(I John 5:14-15)

"And whatever we ask we receive from Him, because we keep His commandments and do those things that are pleasing in His sight."(I John 3:22)

"Because he has set his love upon Me, therefore I will deliver him; I will set him on high, because he has known My name. He shall call upon Me, and I will answer him; I will be with him in trouble; I will deliver him and honor him. With long life I will satisfy him, and show him My salvation." (Psalm 91:14-16)

"It shall come to pass that before they call, I will answer; and while they are still speaking, I will hear."(Isaiah 65:24)

"Then you will call upon Me and go and pray to Me, and I will listen to you. And you will seek Me

and find Me, when you search for Me with all your heart."(Jeremiah 29:12-13)

"Ask, and it will be given to you; seek, and you will find; knock, and it will be opened to you. 8 For everyone who asks receives, and he who seeks finds, and to him who knocks it will be opened. 9 Or what man is there among you who, if his son asks for bread, will give him a stone? 10 Or if he asks for a fish, will he give him a serpent? 11 If you then, being evil, know how to give good gifts to your children, how much more will your Father who is in heaven give good things to those who ask Him!" (Matthew 7:7-11)

"Let my prayer be set before You as incense, the lifting of my hands as the evening sacrifice." (Ps 141:2)

"If you ask anything in My name, I will do it." (John 14:14)

"The effective, fervent prayer of a righteous man avails much." (James 5:16)

NOTE: There are more Scriptures on prayer for you to seek out and add to this list.

Some of us will say that we are too busy or don't know how to communicate with God. And some of us will come up with other excuses.

Well, I hope that your confidence has been built up after reading the Scriptures and now you can put all of your excuses away and begin the process of simple communication.

Listed below are some simple techniques you can apply and begin to establish your simple communication as you regularly seek to be in God's presence.

Simple Communication with God

For your Review:

Do you accept the invitation to communicate with God daily? Explain in detail.

What were some of the excuses you made not to communicate with God?

Did you say the Scriptures out loud? If not, please go back and do it now.

After reading these Scriptures, write the ones that touched your heart.

Journal Your Thoughts:

_____
_____
_____
_____
_____
_____
_____
_____
_____
_____
_____
_____
_____
_____
_____
_____

Journal Your Thoughts:

Journal Your Thoughts:

Journal Your Thoughts:

Journal Your Thoughts:

Journal Your Thoughts:

Journal Your Thoughts:

Journal Your Thoughts:

Simple Communication with God

Journal Your Thoughts:

Journal Your Thoughts:

Journal Your Thoughts:

Journal Your Thoughts:

Journal Your Thoughts:

LET'S GET STARTED

Let's Set The Atmosphere

READY!!!!

1. Find your special meeting place.
2. Make sure your prayer area is clean and fresh
3. Take your bible, pad and pen.
4. Saturate the atmosphere with praise and worship music.

Now you can turn off your praise and worship music and relax so you can have **Simple Communication with God.**

IT'S TIME TO COMMUNICATE!
REMEMBER IT IS A TWO-WAY DIALOGUE

Begin your communication. It's time to communicate with God and praise Him by talking about who He is and all His vast wonders. Tell Him how you appreciate the stars, the moon, the wind and the sun. Tell Him there is no one like Him in the world. Thank Him for waking you up this morning with a sound mind (Amen) and the activities of your limbs. Let Him know you take nothing for granted. Thank Him for your family and extended family members. Confess your sin and any wrong doing. Ask Him for forgiveness and then forgive anyone who has wronged you or hurt you. Release all bitterness, contention, jealousy, anger, negative thoughts, etc. that is not conducive for God to move and answer the petitions or prayers you will communicate to Him.

Now you can begin to pour your heart out to Him regarding all your needs, your family needs, your community needs, etc. Let Him know the trouble that you have endured and ask Him for restoration and strength. Ask Him to open your eyes and increase your faith. End your communication telling the Lord again how good He is.

WAIT ON THE LORD!

Now take time and abide or dwell in His presence so He can share back with you.

What does it mean to Abide or dwell in His Presence?

The term abide means: to reside, place to dwell, place to endure or remain.

The term dwell means to inhabit, live, lodge, remain, or stay. We must make a conscious decision to abide or dwell in God's presence. After we take time and pour out all our problems to Him, then we must take time and relax in His arms and hear what He will share with us. Abiding in His presence allows us to learn God's ways and thoughts. Abiding in His presence allows us to relinquish all our worldly cares that keep us from moving forward in life. We are able to cast our cares on Him knowing He cares for us. Abiding in His presence allows our minds to become clear and focused. Abiding in His presence allows us to reconnect to our Source to get our daily renewal. We can renew our minds, refuel our bodies, and receive restoration and deliverance from anything and everything that is depressing, oppressing or suppressing us. Abiding in His presence allows us to respond instead of react to situations. Our hunger and thirst are quenched in His presence as we love on Him. Abiding in His presence refreshes, nourishes and replenishes our joy, health, and strength. We are renewed with boldness, courage and wisdom.

So take time and just relax. Don't be in a hurry to leave His presence once you've finished communicating. Listen for His still small voice (that often sounds just like your voice) and receive your instructions and directives.

For your Review:

Did you set up a special meeting place with the Lord?

Is this place clean and fresh?

Did you identify your praise and worship music?

How does your meeting place feel to you? Explain in detail.

How does the music change the atmosphere?

How do you feel pouring your heart out to the Lord?

Write down and share how you appreciate the Lord.

Write down and share your expression of why you are thankful.

What does it mean to wait on the Lord?

How do you feel waiting quietly?

Did you have your pen and paper handy to write down what the Lord instructed?

Overall, how did this section assist in you setting the atmosphere and communicating with the Lord? Write a detailed summary.

Journal Your Thoughts:

Journal Your Thoughts:

Make sure you remember to do the following:

KEEP YOUR APPOINTMENT

SCHEDULE a MEETING day and time (if not daily). Decide whether you will meet with God in the morning, afternoon, or evening. NO MATTER WHAT, keep your appointment. It's a date!

SHUT OUT ALL NOISE

FIND a QUIET PLACE away from everyone and everything. Remove all distractions so you can FOCUS solely on God. Clear your mind/thoughts of all the rambling cluttered thoughts from issues you've encountered. Remember no distractions! So turn the phone ringer to off, unhook the doorbell, put the dog outside, tell the children/spouse not to disturb you, etc. This is your time with God. Now that you have identified your quiet place,

LISTEN, GOD HAS SOMETHING TO SHARE WITH YOU

God wants to communicate with you and share instructions on how to get your needs met. He will reveal to you what you must do. It may come in the form of Scriptures, lyrics from a song, or an impression in your spirit man. Don't limit God to how He will speak to you. Be open and alert. Do not be in a hurry! Wait patiently for His still small voice.

JOT DOWN WHAT EVER IS IMPRESSED IN YOUR SPIRIT

WRITE DOWN WHAT YOU SENSE in your spirit man. Were you led to any Scriptures? Were you given any instructions/directives to follow? LISTEN keenly and take notes. This will enable you to review all instructions/directives from the Holy Spirit and follow so you will keep track of answered prayers and dates/times of your simple communication with God. This will become your prayer journal!

Simple Communication with God

For Your Review:

Take some time and write down your thoughts about this section.

Where do you need to make improvement?

Are you ready to write in your journal daily?

Journal Your Thoughts:

_____
_____
_____
_____
_____
_____
_____
_____
_____
_____
_____
_____
_____
_____
_____
_____
_____
_____
_____
_____

Journal Your Thoughts:

Journal Your Thoughts:

Journal Your Thoughts:

Journal Your Thoughts:

Journal Your Thoughts:

Journal Your Thoughts:

Simple Prayers

> *"The LORD is near to all who call upon Him, to all who call upon Him in truth." (Psalm 145:18)*

Lord I thank you that your word tells me that you are near to all who call upon You in truth. I call upon you Jehovah in truth today, for you to cover my family members with the blood of Jesus and keep them safe from all hurt, harm and danger in Jesus' name.

> *"Because he has set his love upon Me, therefore I will deliver him; I will set him on high, because he has known My name. He shall call upon Me, and I will answer him; I will be with him in trouble; I will deliver him and honor him. With long life I will satisfy him, and show him My salvation." (Psalm 91:14-16)*

Lord, I thank you for delivering me out of my desperate situations because I set my love upon You. Thank you for setting me on high, because I have known your name. Whenever I call upon You, You answer. You said that you would be with me in trouble and not only will you deliver me but you will honor me and satisfy me with long life and show me Your salvation. God do it for me today. In Jesus' name. Amen.

> *"Now this is the confidence that we have in Him, that if we ask anything according to His will, He*

hears us. And if we know that He hears us, whatever we ask, we know that we have the petitions that we have asked of Him".(I John 5:14-15)

Lord, God, I thank you for being all that you are to me. Your Word says that I can have confidence that if I ask anything according to your will, you hear me and if you hear me whatever I ask, I know I can have that which I've asked of you. I now petition you on behalf of my neighborhood. I ask that you save the young men and women who are standing on the corners selling, buying and using drugs. God I ask you to deliver them from the hand of the enemy and reveal your light in their lives. I thank you Lord that my neighborhood is safe from the gang bangers, muggers and robbers. Thank you that the senior citizens are safe. Thank you that our young men and women begin to respect themselves and worship you heavenly Father. I plead the blood of Jesus over our neighborhood and thank you in advance for your wisdom, knowledge and understanding of how I can be a light in the midst of darkness. In Jesus' name. Amen

"Pray without ceasing." —(1 Thessalonians 5:17)

Lord God, I thank you for the invitation to pray without ceasing. This gives me the opportunity to communicate with you all day. I have a whole lot to share and can't always find the proper wording, but just being able to share with you is great. I trust you with my inner most thoughts and know you'll direct me accordingly. Lord you see everything that I have encountered today; you see the good and the bad. You heard my laughter and my cries; my good and terrible thoughts, but through it all God I was able to empty my heart out to you and you restored my joy and peace. It's just an honor to share with you. I love and adore you for your availability to hear me. In Jesus' name. Amen.

> "And whatever things you ask in prayer, believing, you will receive." (Matthew 21:22)

Lord, I thank you that you are amazing. You are not a man that you should lie, nor the son of man that you have to repent. I thank you that Your word is truth and whatever things I am asking you for in prayer I will receive because I believe. Lord I believe that you are able to do abundantly above anything I can think or ask. I have communicated the best way I know how, but I also know that you know my heart and see the situations at hand that need your assistance. Thank you for showing me that you heard me and allowing me to increase my faith. In Jesus' name. Amen.

> "Let my prayer be set before You as incense, the lifting of my hands as the evening sacrifice." (Ps 141:2)

Lord, God, I bow in your presence. I have scheduled this appointment to meet you here and want my prayer to rise up to You as incense. Let my prayers be like a sweet smelling savor in your nostrils. I lift up my hands as the evening sacrifice. These are holy hands needing a touch from you. My hands are your hands to be used to heal someone who is in need of healing. My hands are your hands to be used to bless someone that needs a blessing. My hands are your hands to do your will this day. Thy kingdom come, thy will be done in my life as my hands are lifted unto you. Cause my hands to prosper in whatever I do and you get all the glory from my life. In Jesus' name. Amen

> *"Then you will call upon Me and go and pray to Me, and I will listen to you. And you will seek Me and find Me, when you search for Me with all your heart." (Jeremiah 29:12-13)*

Lord, your word says that I will call upon You and pray, and when I do that you will listen to me. Thank you for hearing my prayers. I chose to seek and find you in my daily communication with you. I search for you with all my heart. My heart belongs to you and pants like the deer for the water brook of your presence. I enjoy taking time out to be in your presence and sense your touch. I feel the anointing in the atmosphere. Lord, you are a wonder and peace to my soul. Thank you for allowing me into your throne room and supping at your feet. My life will change after being in your presence. In your presence is fullness of joy and this joy is my strength. Thank you for letting me call upon your name. Your name is powerful, Your name is awesome; Your name is Alpha and Omega, the beginning and the end. In Jesus' name. Amen.

Your *Simple* Prayers can change any ATMOSPHERE From CHAOS to PEACE!

For Your Review:

After reading this section, how do you feel about simple communication with God?

Identify five Scriptures and write a simple prayer for each. Repeat this exercise monthly.

Journal Your Thoughts:

Journal Your Thoughts:

Journal Your Thoughts:

Journal Your Thoughts:

Journal Your Thoughts:

Journal Your Thoughts:

Journal Your Thoughts:

Simple Prayer Declarations

I now have confidence that my simple communication with God will change the atmosphere and cause positive change to happen. I open my mouth and decree things and they are established according to the Word of God. I make these declarations by faith.

I spend 15 or more minutes a day in my quiet place.

I know my relationship with God is growing.

I have what I say according to the Word of God.

I believe my prayers are answered.

I am open and free to have simple communications with God.

My heart is pure and honest.

My confidence is in the Lord.

My love is set upon the Lord.

I pray for my family, friends, neighborhood and myself daily.

I am a living witness for the Lord Jesus Christ.

I walk in the light of the Word.

I am a gatekeeper for my family and community.

I put on the whole armor of God so that I can stand against the wiles of the devil.

I am strong in the Lord and in the power of His might.

(Feel free to add to this list as led by the Holy Spirit)

Simple Communication with God

For Your Review:

Write seven prayer declarations on an index card and repeat at least three times daily.

Journal Your Thoughts:

Journal Your Thoughts:

Journal Your Thoughts:

Journal Your Thoughts:

Simple Communication With God
is also available in large print"
and E-Book format

For bookings and other information contact
Dr. Dawn Dixon at:

P.O. Box 438988
Chicago, IL 60643

Email: dr.dawndixon@yahoo.com

www.unveilingrosesministries.com
www.facebook.com/Dr.Dawn

Phone: 773-264-8487

About the Author

Have you ever been asked to pray for someone and said "I'll pray when I get home"? You said you'd do it later because you felt inadequate to communicate with God at that moment. My book will teach and assist you in praying with simplicity, getting answers to your prayers and the prayers of other people when they ask you. It will enhance your confidence in God and your ability to communicate with Him daily. Get Ready and BE READY to simply communicate your needs, desires, and passions to the Lord using these simple techniques.

Dr. Dixon is the Overseer of Unveiling Roses Ministries. A ministry established to educate, empower and enhance individuals who have been discouraged and distracted from God's purpose. She is a loving and caring person who believes that God is Awesome and Almighty, filled with Grace and Mercy toward His children. She also believes that He desires for all of His children to become and be the best they can. She knows that God is no shorter than His Word written in Jeremiah 29:11..."for I know the thoughts and plans that I have for you, says the Lord, thoughts and plans for welfare and peace and not for evil, to give you hope in your final outcome. "

Her belief as a Minister of the Gospel is to continually share the Good News and encourage people that there is hope beyond what they see in the natural. Dr. Dixon shows the best way to escape into the loving arms of our Heavenly Father who waits daily for us to seek Him for an intimate encounter. She teaches Kingdom principles, simple communication with God through prayer as well as other kingdom messages that can change the mindset or paradigm of individuals. She is a genuine and true worshipper who loves entering into the presence of God and communing with Him daily.

God has blessed her to accomplish the following: Doctorate of Philosophy; Masters in Criminal Justice; Bachelors in Church Ministry and an Associate in Christian Studies. She also holds the following certifications: reflexologist, criminal justice specialist, Effective Black Parent Trainer and Christian Counselor. Her mission and vision are to see the down trodden raised up through the resurrection power of Jesus Christ, and become living epistles to show the world that God is real and alive today!

"The Lord is near to all who call upon Him." Psalm 145:18

www.ingramcontent.com/pod-product-compliance
Lightning Source LLC
Chambersburg PA
CBHW071831290426
44109CB00017B/1796